25
Christmas
FAMILY DEVOTIONS
AND ACTIVITIES

BRETT A. BELL

ISBN: 1539729796
ISBN-13: 978-1539729792

Christmas can be an exciting yet busy time of the year. Between parties, plays, parades, school gatherings, banquets, practices, recitals, traveling, church events, and putting up decorations; it can be exhausting. In all of the confusion, we sometimes lose focus of the true meaning of Christmas. While presents, lights, and vacations are nice, they are not the reason for the season. The reason is Jesus Christ and the gift He brings to all those who believe.

This book is a tool to help families spend time together each day focusing on why Jesus' birth is so important. As you gather together, have someone read aloud the specified Scripture from the Bible. The brief devotion can then be read. These devotions are written so that both the young and old can understand. Your family may then choose to share your reactions to the Bible verse(s). A time of family prayer should follow.

After each devotion, there is an optional activity. Some of the activities are very simple and easy. Others require a bit of preparation and/or small expense. Feel free to look ahead to ensure that you will have everything you need each day.

It has been said that children spell love T-I-M-E. Help your family grow in God's grace by spending time together each day. As you do, you will be ensuring that your children not only know God's Word, but that they love it also.

DECEMBER
1

Read: John 1:14

Jesus has many names in the Bible. Sometimes He is called the Christ, the Son, or the Messiah. In this verse, He is known as the Word. Maybe you have heard the Bible called the Word of God before.

Since Adam and Eve, God had promised that He would send someone to save us. Over and over again, the Bible reminds us of that promise. However, for a long time, people waited and Jesus never came. Some people probably questioned whether or not a Saviour would really ever come. Then one day it happened. God's Word came true. Jesus, the promised Saviour, became a man. He looked like us. He talked like us. He ate, drank, laughed, and cried just like us. Yet, even though He was 100% man, He was also 100% God (see John 1:1). Real people just like us were able to see, hear, and touch God.

More important than that, Jesus had come to pay for our sins by dying on the cross. That is what makes Christmas so important. He had the birthday, but we got the gift. That is the greatest gift we could ever hope to get. It is the gift of eternal life by placing our faith and trust in Jesus the Son of God.

Read a Christmas themed book together as a family.

DECEMBER 2

Read: Matthew 1:18

Mary was relatively young when she found out that she was going to give birth to Jesus. At the time, she was planning to get married to a man named Joseph. Many people wondered who the child's father was. Joseph knew that he was not the father. This caused him to be confused and possibly angry too. Thankfully, God helped Joseph to understand that the baby's father was not another man. Rather, the new baby was the Son of God.

This was an incredible miracle and blessing. Mary was excited about her new baby, and so was Joseph. However, some people did not believe that the baby Jesus was God's Son. These people could not understand how a girl like Mary could have God's child. Nevertheless, Mary had faith that God would give her strength to be a good mother to baby Jesus.

There are some people today who still do not believe that Mary gave birth to God's Son. Christmas is a great time to remind us to pray for those people we know who do not believe in Jesus Christ.

Call someone who may be lonely this Christmas and sing them a Christmas carol together as a family.

DECEMBER 3

Read: Matthew 1:21

Close your eyes and think about Christmas. What pops into your head? Some people might think of presents, food, family gatherings, or a warm fire. Did you picture a baby in a manger? That baby's name is Jesus. Of course, Jesus was not just an ordinary baby. He was God's Son.

God had a great plan for His Son. A plan to save His people from their sins. With all of the celebrations going on this time of year, it is easy to forget about sin. When we break God's commands, we call that sin. Sins are always bad no matter how big or how small. In fact, sins are so bad that God must punish us for them. Have you ever done something bad? If so, then God knows about it.

Many people hope that God will forget about their sins. However, the Bible teaches us that God cannot simply ignore our sins. That would make God unjust. So, in order to help us, God had to make a way to save us from our sins. He did that by sending his Son, Jesus. Thank God today that He loves you so much that He gave His Son to save you from your sins.

Give a gift to Jesus. Get out some wrapping paper and a box. Discuss what you think Jesus would mostly like for Christmas. One of Jesus' greatest desires is our personal holiness (Eph. 5:27). Write on a piece of paper some sin or addiction in your life that you need to give to Jesus. This can be kept a secret if you wish. Then put the paper in a box and wrap the present. Keep it in plain view for the remainder of the season. Don't forget to write "to Jesus" on the tag. Every time you look at the gift remind yourself that you cannot be holy without the Lord's strength and help. Rest in His power and grace this Christmas.

DECEMBER
4

Read: Isaiah 7:14

Whose birthday do we celebrate on Christmas? If you said Jesus, then you are right. However, the Bible gives us many names for Jesus. One of those names is Immanuel.

Maybe you have heard of the Christmas song, "O Come, O Come Immanuel." The name Immanuel literally means, God with us. Many people believe that Jesus was a good man. They might even say He was a good teacher. Other people say that He did a lot of good things. However, numerous people do not understand one of the most important things about Jesus. He was God in the flesh (Jn. 10:30). When Mary was holding Jesus in her arms, she was holding God. The people that came to see Jesus were looking at God.

Christmas is such a wonderful holiday because it helps us to celebrate God's love for us. He loves us so much that He left heaven to be with us. More importantly, He wants us to be with Him. In order to be with Him, we needed to be saved from our sins. Jesus died on the cross to pay the penalty for our sins. When we accept the gift of salvation by faith in Jesus Christ, we get the greatest present we could ever hope for. We get to be together with God forever.

Talk with your family about the joys of simply spending this season together as a family. Talk about those you know who might not have family around. Consider inviting that person to your home to celebrate one of your family traditions with you.

DECEMBER
5

Read: Matthew 2:1-2

Strange things can happen in the sky. Sometimes the sun turns black. Sometimes the moon turns red. Sometimes stars appear to fall from the sky. The year Jesus was born, an unusual star appeared in the sky. Many people around knew about this particular star. Yet, very few knew why it had appeared.

Some wise men from the east had been reading the Bible and watching the skies. They knew that Jesus was going to be born soon. When they saw the star, they knew it was a sign that He had finally come. When they finally arrived in Israel, they assumed that everyone knew about the birth of Jesus. They also assumed that the Jewish people would be excited about it. What they learned was quite the opposite. Most of the Jews did not know and did not care. Isn't it sad that some people who should be the closest to God are sometimes the furthest away?

The truth is that there are no excuses when it comes to knowing Jesus. Some people are raised going to church and still don't really know Jesus. Other people were raised in homes that hated God and yet they are very close to Him. The wise men didn't let anything stop them from getting close to Jesus. Neither should you.

Go outside tonight and look at the stars. Talk about the unusual nature of the star that led the wise men to Bethlehem. See if your children can find any patterns or shapes in the stars. Remind them that people have been looking at those same stars for thousands of years. The book of Job in the Bible even mentions constellations. As you look into the heavens, be encouraged by the fact that Jesus is coming again soon!

DECEMBER 6

Read: Micah 5:2

Being small can be frustrating. However, many good things come in small packages. Bethlehem was considered a small city. Especially when people compared it to the nearby Jerusalem. Jerusalem had the temple of God. Jerusalem is where the religious leaders lived. Jerusalem had more wealth and power. Nevertheless, God chose Bethlehem to be the birthplace of his Son, Jesus.

The most important person to ever be born into this world was Jesus. In Micah 5:2, we are told something surprising about Jesus. He was very old. While He looked and acted like a normal baby, He was anything but normal. That is because Jesus didn't begin life as a baby. In fact, He never began life. That is because He is eternal. In other words, He has always lived.

At Christmas, we celebrate the time that God the Son became a baby. The next time you look at a manger, see if you can find the baby Jesus. Then remind yourself that even though baby Jesus was small, He was also very special.

Get a manger scene and place all of the pieces to the side. Place the figures into their correct positions one by one. Explain the Bible character each figure represents. Put the baby Jesus figure last. Make it a point to emphasize how all of the figures are centered around Jesus Christ.

DECEMBER 7

Read: Genesis 22:7-8

Have you ever had to wait a long time for something exciting? It seems that the best things in life require patience. God made Abraham wait until he was 100 years old to have a son. That is a long time. When Isaac was finally born, Abraham was very happy.

After several years, God asked Abraham to do something strange. He asked him to give up his son as a sacrifice to God. Abraham loved his son, but he loved God more. So he did what God told him to do. Abraham told Isaac to come with him in order to give God a sacrifice. Isaac didn't understand that he was going to be the sacrifice. As they were walking, Isaac asked his dad where the lamb was that they would be giving to God. Then Abraham told his son that God would provide a lamb for himself. Do you know that is exactly what God did? God told Abraham that he did not actually want him to sacrifice his son. He only wanted to see if Abraham really loved him.

Do you know how to tell if someone loves you? They will be willing to give you something that is very special to them. That is just what God did on Christmas day. He gave us His only begotten Son. That's how we know that God loves us very much.

Make homemade Christmas cards and pray about who God would want you to give them to.

DECEMBER 8

Read: Philippians 2:5-7

Has anyone ever given you a compliment? It feels good when people recognize positive things about us. After all, you are a very special person. God made you in His image. You are fearfully and wonderfully made.

Jesus was a very special person too. He was smarter, stronger, funnier, wiser, and more talented than anyone else. Before He was born in Bethlehem, He lived in heaven. While there, he had servants, treasures, and everything was always perfect. However, He left all the things He had to become more like us. He left His throne in heaven. He left all of the angels who worshiped Him. He gave up His perfect body to be made into the likeness of a man. Once He came into the world, many people did not like Him very much. He was also poor. His body was not as strong either. The King had to become a Servant. It was the only way to be able to give us the gift of eternal life.

The Bible teaches us to be willing to be a servant just like Jesus. Even though we are special, we should not let that stop us from doing things for others. Christmas is the perfect time of the year to look for opportunities to serve others.

Make paper snowflakes by folding white pieces of paper and cutting out random shapes. Talk about how each one is unique. Remind one another that each person is created by God. Like snowflakes, we are all different. We are also all loved and valued equally by God no matter what our achievements are.

DECEMBER
9

Read: Isaiah 6:9

Have you ever been in charge of something important? Sometimes it is fun to be the boss. However, other times it is very hard. The more people you are in charge of, the harder it can be.

Even individuals who are very good at leading, sometimes make mistakes. Presidents and kings mess up occasionally. Teachers and principals don't do everything perfectly. Also, dads and moms get some things wrong. We all make mistakes, and that is okay. Mistakes are God's way of teaching us how much we need Him.

The Bible teaches us that Jesus is going to be the king of the whole world. That is what it means when it says that the government shall be upon His shoulder [KJV]. In His kingdom, everything will be wonderful. He will not make mistakes like we do. When God is in charge, everything becomes perfect.

Thankfully, we do not need to wait until Jesus comes again to make Him our king. When we submit to Him and serve Him, then He is already our king. Have you been serving Jesus with your whole heart?

Play a board game together as a family. Point out the importance of following the instruction in a game. When you follow the rules, then everyone has fun. The same is true when we follow God's commands.

DECEMBER 10

Read: Galatians 4:4,5

Some people are born into wealthy families. Other people are born into humble households. Each type of family has its own advantages. At Christmas, we celebrate the birth of Jesus Christ into the world. His earthly parents were modest people. Joseph was a carpenter. That means that he helped to build things in order to make a living. He earned enough money to support his family with food, clothes, and a home. However, they did not live in a palace. They were a regular working class family.

Have you ever wondered why God didn't give Jesus' family more money? Doesn't God's Son deserve the very best? He could have had the finest clothes, toys, and furniture. He could have had servants who did anything He asked them to do. But instead, God chose to have Jesus live an average life. He was born of a woman. He lived under the law. He fulfilled the law. Finally, He died under the law so that we might be redeemed. Give thanks to God for letting His Son take our place not only in life but also in death.

Get some building blocks, Legos, or other construction type toys. If you don't have any of these toys, then get creative with items you have around the house. Work together to make one or more of the following Christmas themed scenes.

- A Manger

- Bethlehem

- A Church Building

- A Home with Decorations

DECEMBER 11

Read: Psalms 107:1

Do you have a wish list for Christmas? How many presents do you think you will receive? Will you get every single item on your wish list? Most of us will not get everything we want. Not in Christmas and not in life.

Occasionally, we get discouraged when we think about all of the things that we want but do not have. We might even talk to other people who have more than us. This can make us feel like we are not as important as the people who have more than we do.

However, that is not the way God sees things. God does not show His love for us by getting us everything we ask for. You see, His gifts are better than the ones we usually request. Sometimes God gives us a loving family. Sometimes God gives us patience and understanding. Other times God gives us excitement and adventure. Still, other times He gives us important life experiences. That is because God is more interested in teaching us how to be satisfied with what we do have rather than spoiled.

Learn to be satisfied with all of the gifts God has chosen to give you. Tell Him how thankful you are to know that He loves you and wants to give you the very best.

Jesus gave up a lot when He left heaven. However, He was not upset by it. Rather, He wanted to give those things up in order to save us. This teaches us about the importance of people over things. Material things can never make us truly fulfilled or happy. Have a talk with your family about cutting back your Christmas spending this year. Joy should come from Jesus, not presents.

DECEMBER 12

Read: Romans 6:23

What is your favorite type of wrapping paper? Most people have never considered what type they like best. Instead, we usually just rip into it without a thought. No one calls his or her grandmother on Christmas afternoon to tell her about the wonderful wrapping paper their gift came in.

The best part about a gift isn't the wrapping paper or the box. The best part about a gift is that it is free. Otherwise, it is not a gift. The Bible teaches us that God has a very special gift that He wants everyone to have. That gift is eternal life. Eternal life means that we will live with God forever.

Right now, we do not get to see God. We cannot give Him a hug or even a telephone call. However, one day that will all change. We will be with God forever. Not because we were good. Not because we went to church on Sundays. Not because we were baptized. Rather because we accepted the gift of eternal life through Jesus Christ.

Notice that this verse ends with an important word – "Lord [KJV]." We do not need to behave a certain way in order to go to heaven. Yet, we do desire to act a certain way because Jesus is our Lord. He loves us, and we love Him. Because we love Him and because He is our God, then we do what He wants us to do. Some people have heard about Jesus many times but have never accepted His gift of eternal life. Have you ever accepted His gift?

Have each member of the family take turns telling about the greatest gift they have ever received. Ask them what makes that gift so special. Was the gift free? Could you have obtained the gift by yourself?

DECEMBER 13

Read: James 1:17

Where does your food come from? Many people get their food from a market or store. They take their money and buy what they need each week. Why then do we thank God for our food? Why don't we thank ourselves for earning our food, homes, and other possessions?

The answer is found in John 15:5 where Jesus says, "...without me ye can do nothing [KJV]." The Bible teaches us to work and earn a living. However, it is God who gives us the ability to work. He causes the sun to rise and fall. He brings the rain that waters the garden. He makes the food. We simply harvest it. He also provides the strength in our arms and legs to work. He gives us the ability to think and know. He teaches our eyes to see and our hearts to beat. He gives breath to our lungs.

Everything we have in life comes from Him and Him alone. Each day is filled with God's goodness and blessings. Do not take the small things for granted.

Gather blankets and various furniture items to make an indoor tent/fort. Make sure it is big enough for the whole family. Talk about how thankful you are to have the home and things God has provided to your family.

DECEMBER 14

Read: Psalm 72:11

What is your favorite Christmas carol? Have you ever heard of the song, "We Three Kings?" This hymn is based on the story of the wise men who visited Jesus when He was very young.

The Bible never says exactly how many wise men there were. However, it does mention three gifts that they brought to Jesus. They were gold, frankincense, and myrrh. When the wise men found little Jesus, they all fell down and worshiped Him. We don't know much about these wise men. However, we do know that they were wealthy and important people. They traveled a long way just to see Jesus. Their story teaches us that Jesus is the most important person in all of history. Even the rich and powerful bow down and serve Him.

There will be a day when EVERYONE falls down on their knees and submits to Jesus' authority as God and King. Look around this Christmas season at all of the lights, decorations, and celebrations. Listen to the Christmas music. Enjoy the time spent with family and friends. Let all of these things be a reminder to us about how important Jesus' birth really is.

Get in the car and drive around town looking at all of the Christmas decorations. Talk about which ones you like the most and why. Be sure to include how some simple decorations can be more meaningful than the elaborate ones. Explain how Jesus' birth was simple and humble.

DECEMBER 15

Read: Isaiah 9:2

The dark can be scary even for adults. God uses darkness to describe things that are not holy. When Jesus was born, many people were living in darkness. Their lives were not filled with joy or happiness. The things they tried to do to make themselves happy only made things worse. Their lives were so dark that they didn't even know how to obey God.

One day Jesus came and started teaching them about God. At first, everyone was surprised. They couldn't understand why God would send Jesus to people who were living in darkness. Jesus explained that these are the people who needed Him most of all (Lk. 5:31). He came to them in order to help them. He shined a bright light so that they might see God's glory.

Christmas reminds us that we all need the light of Jesus every day. Even when we are good, we still need Him to give light to our lives. Do you know someone who is living in darkness today? Pray about how Jesus might use you to brighten up their life.

Have an old-fashioned Christmas. For one hour tonight, pretend that your home does not have electricity. Get out some candles or a lantern and turn off all the lights. Spend this time together as a family. Play a board game, sing together, tell funny stories, etc.

DECEMBER 16

Read: Luke 2:4,5

Do you know where you were born? Many people do not live in the same city they were born in. That is true about Jesus. His mother and Joseph lived in a city called Nazareth. Then, when Jesus was about to be born, they had to make an important business trip. Mary was going to give birth to Jesus very soon. However, they were forced to travel to a city called Bethlehem in order to pay a special tax.

At the time, this probably felt like a very big problem for Mary and Joseph. They would have been worried and stressed. They would have feared for the health of Mary and the soon to be born baby Jesus. However, God knew exactly what was going to happen. He had foretold that His Son would be born in Bethlehem and He was making it come to pass.

Sometimes our Christmas events don't go as planned. When that happens, just remember Mary and Joseph. God took care of them, and He will take care of you too.

Get a Christmas themed puzzle to do together as a family (simple or elaborate). Enjoy working together as a family on a project. Talk about how life can sometimes be complicated. Jesus came to help us put the pieces of our lives together. When he is in the center of our lives, everything begins to come together.

DECEMBER 17

Read: Luke 2:7

Have you ever traveled during Christmas? Sometimes it can be crowded. That was the case on the very first Christmas. Joseph and Mary had to travel to Bethlehem for some important business. Many other people had to travel for the same reason. When they came into the town, there was no room for them to stay. The only place they could find to sleep was a cattle stall. This was a place where farm animals were kept. It was probably not the cleanest place. It also probably had a smell.

While they were staying there, Mary gave birth to Jesus. We might think that this is a terrible way for God's Son to be born. They should have given Him a palace. He should have had a golden crib. There should have been the softest blankets to wrap Him in. But to God, a manger was perfect.

Jesus was humble. He did not care about riches and gold. He had everything He needed and nothing more. Do you have the things you need? Do you have food, love, shelter, and warmth? Consider yourself blessed.

Have a family sleepover tonight all together in one room. Discuss how crowded it would have been in Bethlehem during the time Jesus was born.

DECEMBER 18

Read: Luke 2:10

Do you ever give presents to other people at Christmas time? Chances are, you put a little tag on each gift that says who they are for. Usually, each gift goes to a different person. One gift for mom. One gift for dad. One gift for grandma, and so on.

If you think about it, Jesus is a type of Christmas gift. He was wrapped in swaddling clothes. He was given on Christmas day. He brings joy to all who receive Him. So where is Jesus' tag and what does it say? Instead of a tag, God used an angel to tell us who the gift of Jesus was for. Look at the last three words of Luke 2:10. It says, "...to all people [KJV]."

Jesus is a Christmas gift for everyone. You do not need to be special to receive Jesus. You do not need to be rich or poor. You do not need to be small or big. You do not need to have a certain type of family. It doesn't even matter if you've been naughty or nice. Jesus is a gift that God wants to give everyone. That includes you.

Have everyone put their name on a small piece of paper. Secretly draw names. Agree to pray for that person throughout the week.

DECEMBER 19

Read: Luke 2:11

Waiting can be hard. Christmas day only comes once a year. We look at the calendar and circle the date. But it always seems to take a long time to finally arrive. The same can be said about Jesus' birth.

God promised that a Saviour would be born. He told Adam and Eve. He told Abraham, Moses, David, and Isaiah. The people of Israel knew He was coming, but it felt like it was taking forever. Then suddenly, Jesus was born. Christ the Lord appeared as a little baby in the city of David called Bethlehem.

The shepherds who first heard this message were surprised to hear it. Sure, they knew Jesus was supposed to be coming. But they didn't know exactly when. Once they realized what was happening, they were probably excited. Remember the shepherds while you are waiting for Christmas day.

It is exciting to open presents, visit with family, and enjoy good food. However, it is much more exciting to know that a Saviour was given to the world the day Jesus was born. Let the excitement of knowing Jesus Christ stay in your heart every day of the year.

Take turns sharing your favorite Christmas memory with one another.

DECEMBER 20

Read: Luke 2:13

Have you ever been to a celebration? We often celebrate weddings, graduations, promotions, and anniversaries. After all, good things deserve a celebration.

The day the angel announced the birth of Jesus, there was a celebration in heaven. The angels in heaven were excited to praise God for sending His Son Jesus to be their Saviour. They were not ashamed to worship God for His goodness and love. They gave glory and praise to their God.

Christmas is a great reminder to us all about how wonderful it is to have Jesus in our lives. Jesus brought with Him peace and good will to us all. For that, He deserves praise. Not just during Christmas but all year long.

Activity

Have a family celebration. Put on or make festive hats. Sing Christmas carols together. Make your own music or cue a Christmas music playlist through your favorite electronic device. Put out a few simple snacks and have a good time.

DECEMBER 21

Read: Luke 2:17

The shepherds heard about the birth of Jesus from the angel. After they had heard, they obeyed. Their search for Jesus led them to the manger where he lay. Everything the angel had said was true. Their encounter with the real live Jesus is something that few others had experienced. It was a visit that changed their lives forever.

Have you ever met Jesus Christ? He is no longer a baby in a manger, but He still wants you to know Him. If you already know Jesus, then you know how exciting it was the day you trusted Him as Saviour. It was a day that changed your life forever.

After the shepherds had seen Jesus, they went and told everyone they could about what they had heard and seen. That is how easy it is to tell someone about Jesus. You don't need to know everything about the Bible. All you need to know is what you have seen and heard. We call this our testimony.

Christmas is a great time to be outgoing with your faith. Let others know that you are excited about the gift of Jesus Christ. Tell them about His glory. Tell them about His peace. Tell them about the gift of eternal life.

Make a sweet Christmas treat and give it/them away to those who you think could use a little Christmas cheer.

DECEMBER 22

Read: Luke 2:19

Sometimes life goes by very quickly. As soon as the Christmas decorations get put out, it seems it is time to take them down. Then, all we have left are the memories.

The day Jesus was born was a big day for Mary. She was tired. She had entertained visitors who told her stories about angels. She was sleeping in a cattle stall. Yet, most of all, she was holding God's Son in her arms. It was a lot to take in. Once the company left and the commotion died down, she was left alone to think. She probably wondered why she was chosen to be Jesus' mother. She probably wondered how she could possibly raise someone so important. She was probably full of joy and full of fear. But most of all, she was probably full of wonder. After all, Jesus wasn't just another baby. He was God in the flesh.

It is a special moment when we realize that Jesus isn't just another story. He isn't just another holiday. He isn't just another fairy tale character. He is the Creator of all the world and universe, and He wants to have a relationship with you. This Christmas is a great time to remember that God loves you and wants your love in return.

Watch a Christmas movie together as a family. Don't forget the popcorn.

DECEMBER 23

Read: Luke 2:20

Do you remember the best day of your life? For many people, it was the day they got saved. There is a joy that comes from knowing the Lord. It is a joy unspeakable and full of glory. That means it is so good that it's hard to describe with words.

When someone trusts Jesus as Saviour, they often want to tell everyone they know. They can't help but smile everywhere they go. They have a feeling of peace like they have never known. It is different from any other feeling. That's because being saved is more about a filling than a feeling. God is invited into your life, and He begins to make changes. He fills you with the Holy Spirit.

The shepherds met baby Jesus, and they were changed forever. Yet, it all started with a message they had heard. Have you heard the message of Jesus? Have you seen God moving in the lives of others? If so, then give God praise and glory for all the things you have heard and seen.

Treat yourselves to hot chocolate or warm apple cider. Discuss how the hot beverage helps to warm us up on the inside. Tell your family that Jesus warms us on the inside too. Try to describe how we should invite Jesus into our lives and our hearts (Eph. 3:17) to change us and make us more like Him.

DECEMBER 24

Read: Luke 2:30

Raise your hand if you have seen Jesus. The truth is that Jesus has been in heaven for a long time now. No one has seen Him for quite a while. But that hasn't always been the case.

A man named Simeon was worshiping God in the temple in Jerusalem one day. He was an elderly man that God had given a promise to. The Holy Spirit had told him that he would not die until he had seen Jesus with his own eyes. One day, God delivered on His promise. Simeon was blessed to be able to see Jesus with his own eyes.

That is a privilege few have enjoyed. The great thing about this story is that God always delivers on His promises. Sometimes we may have to wait longer than we want but He is always faithful. We don't need to see Jesus with our eyes to know that He is real. By faith, we believe in the promises of the Bible. Just like Simeon, we place our trust in God. We may have to wait a while. However, one day the promise will come. Just like Simeon, we will see God's salvation. We will see Jesus face to face.

Enjoy a candy cane snack. Discuss how the candy cane reminds us of Jesus.

- The candy cane looks like a letter J for Jesus.

- If you hold it upside down it looks like a shepherd's crook.

- The white color symbolizes purity and holiness.

- The stripes represent Jesus being whipped (Isa. 53:5).

- The red color symbolizes Jesus' blood that makes us pure.

DECEMBER 25

Read: John 3:16

Does it make you feel good to give gifts? When we love someone, we want to make them happy. Giving gifts is one way that we can do that. We save our money and try to find the perfect gift. We search the store to find the perfect item. Then we can hardly wait to see their reaction when they open our present.

God loves you so much that He wanted to get you the greatest gift anyone has ever received. This gift would cost Him more than anyone has ever paid. It would be the most expensive thing ever given. And He wants you to have it this Christmas.

The gift is Jesus Christ. When you receive Jesus as your Saviour, then you receive the greatest present of all. God has been waiting with excitement to give you this gift. How will you respond?

Christmas can be one of the most selfish days of the year. We often focus on what we want and what we might get. When all of the gifts are opened, we may desire to go our separate ways. Make a commitment to celebrate Christmas day together as a family. Love one another and enjoy being together. This is also a good time to forgive any hurt feeling that may have developed throughout the year. Have a merry Christmas!

Brett A. Bell is a father of five and the pastor of Gant Lake Baptist Church in Florida. He and his wife Amanda have been married since 2003. They work together to create resources to assist others in their daily walk with Christ.

The devotions in this book come from a conservative biblical viewpoint.

Connect with Brett on Facebook
www.facebook.com/nowistheday

Listen to teaching podcasts
gantlake.buzzsprout.com

Other resources available

| Simple Sermon Notes for Kids Ages 7 - 12 | Simple Sermon Notes – A Journal (small) | Sermon Notes Journal for Ladies (larger) |

Connect with Amanda
www.newlifeovernight.com

Made in the USA
San Bernardino, CA
08 December 2016